Traditional
FARMHOUSE COOKING

by Sue Ashworth

Illustrated by Magda Lazou

This is a Siena Book
Siena is an imprint of Parragon
Queen Street House
4 Queen Street
Bath BA1 1HE
Reprinted in 1999

ISBN 0-75253-111-5

Edited, designed and typeset by Haldane Mason, London
Editor: Joanna Swinnerton

Printed in Italy

Note: Cup measurements in this book are for American cups. Tablespoons are assumed to be 15ml. Unless otherwise stated, milk is assumed to be full-fat, eggs are standard size 2 and pepper is freshly ground black pepper.

CONTENTS

LEEK AND POTATO SOUP

---

30 g/1 oz/2 tbsp butter

....

**500 g/1 lb leeks, trimmed and
sliced**

....

1 onion, chopped

....

**900 ml/1½ pints/3½ cups chicken
or vegetable stock**

....

**350 g/12 oz potatoes, peeled and
cut into chunks**

....

1 tbsp chopped fresh chives

....

300 ml/½ pint/1¼ cups milk

....

4 tbsp whipping cream

....

salt and pepper

....

chopped fresh chives to garnish

*This deliciously smooth soup can be served hot in
chilly weather or cold in the summer months, when it
makes a refreshing starter.*

1 Melt the butter in a
large saucepan and
add the leeks and onion.
Cook over a low heat,
stirring frequently, for
about 10 minutes until the
vegetables are softened but not
browned.

2 Add the chicken or vegetable
stock, potatoes and chives.
Bring to the boil, then reduce
the heat, cover and
simmer gently
for 20–30
minutes, until
the vegetables
are cooked.

3 Rub the soup through a
sieve (strainer), or place
in a food processor
or blender and
work until it is
smooth, then
return it to the saucepan. Add
the milk and reheat the soup
gently, stirring occasionally,
until it is piping hot. Season
to taste.

4 If you are serving the soup
hot, whip the cream while
the soup is reheating until the
cream thickens slightly. Ladle
into 4 warmed soup bowls,
spoon an equal amount of

whipped cream on top of each serving and sprinkle with chopped fresh chives.

5 If serving chilled, cool the soup quickly and refrigerate for 2–3 hours until it is ice cold. Add the whipped cream and chives just before serving.

SPLIT PEA AND HAM SOUP

A bowlful of this chunky golden soup on a cold winter's day is almost a meal in itself.

1 Melt the butter or margarine in a large saucepan. Add the onion and carrot and fry gently over a medium heat until the vegetables are softened, about 5 minutes.

2 Stir in the cubes of gammon (bacon) and the cumin and cook gently for a further 5 minutes, stirring frequently.

3 Pour in the ham or vegetable stock and add the yellow split peas. Bring to the boil, then reduce the heat. Cover and simmer the soup very gently for about 45 minutes until the peas are cooked.

4 Add the parsley to the soup and stir well. Season to taste. Ladle into warmed soup bowls and garnish with sprigs of parsley. Serve at once.

POTTED STILTON

This creamy appetizer is a must for blue-cheese lovers. If tightly wrapped and stored in the refrigerator, it will keep for up to 2 weeks.

SERVES ❻

125 g/4 oz/½ cup butter, at room temperature

350 g/12 oz/3 cups blue Stilton cheese, crumbled

60 g/2 oz/1 cup fresh white breadcrumbs

1 tbsp port

1 tsp chopped fresh parsley

1 Put the butter into a large mixing bowl and beat until it is softened. Add the crumbled Stilton cheese and beat together until it is creamy, but not too smooth.

2 Work the breadcrumbs into the cheese mixture, then add the port and parsley. Mix together until thoroughly combined.

3 Pack the mixture into an earthenware pot or other container. Cover and refrigerate.

4 Take the potted Stilton out of the refrigerator about 30 minutes before serving to allow it to reach room temperature. Serve with crackers or fresh, crusty bread.

TWO-CHEESE RAREBIT

For a simple, filling snack, a tasty rarebit is hard to beat. Cream cheese and mature (sharp) Cheddar are combined in this recipe to give a bubbly golden topping.

1 To make the rarebit mixture, put the cream cheese and butter into a large mixing bowl and beat together until blended. Add the grated Cheddar cheese, Worcestershire sauce, chives and chilli powder, and mix well until thoroughly combined.

2 Toast the bread lightly on both sides and spread each piece with the rarebit mixture. Place under a preheated hot grill (broiler) and cook until the topping is melted and bubbling.

Watch the toast carefully as it cooks, as the cheese can burn very quickly.

3 Top each piece with tomato slices and sprinkle with the chopped chives. Serve at once.

CHEESE AND ONION PIE

The simplest of ingredients make a very tasty double-crust savoury pie, delicious served with a crisp salad and sliced tomatoes.

SERVES ❹

500 g/1 lb onions, sliced

175 g/6 oz/1½ cups mature (sharp) Cheddar cheese, grated

300 g/10 oz/2½ cups plain (all-purpose) flour

90 g/3 oz/⅓ cup butter or hard margarine, chilled

60 g/2 oz/¼ cup lard (shortening), chilled

1 tbsp milk

salt and pepper

1 Cook the onions in boiling, lightly salted water for about 10 minutes until tender. Drain thoroughly and mash with a potato masher. Add the grated cheese and mix well. Season to taste and allow to cool.

2 Sift the flour and a pinch of salt into a large mixing bowl. Cut the butter or margarine and lard (shortening) into pieces. Add to the flour and rub in with your fingertips until the mixture resembles fine breadcrumbs. Add enough chilled water to make a firm dough. Knead lightly for a few moments, then wrap and refrigerate for about 10 minutes.

3 Roll out half the dough on a lightly floured work surface (counter) and use to line a 20 cm/8 inch metal pie plate. Spoon the cheese and onion mixture on top. Roll out the remaining dough, moisten the edges with a little water and use to cover the pie. Press the edges together to seal, then trim them. Use any leftover trimmings to make leaves

to garnish the top. Brush with milk to glaze.

4 Place in a preheated oven at 220°C, 425°F, Gas Mark 7, and bake for 10 minutes, then reduce the temperature to 190°C, 375°F, Gas Mark 5 and bake for a further 20–25 minutes until cooked and golden brown.

COUNTRY VEGETABLE AND BARLEY CASSEROLE

This fresh vegetable casserole makes a good accompaniment to meat or poultry, but is also a very satisfying meal by itself.

SERVES ❹

1 tbsp vegetable oil

30 g/1 oz/2 tbsp butter

175 g/6 oz shallots

175 g/6 oz baby carrots

175 g/6 oz baby parsnips

175 g/6 oz small turnips, quartered

350 g/12 oz small new potatoes

60 g/2 oz/¼ cup pearl barley

600 ml/1 pint/2½ cups vegetable stock

300 ml/½ pint/1¼ cups dry white wine

1 tbsp chopped mixed fresh herbs

125 g/4 oz sugar snap peas or mangetout (snow peas)

salt and pepper

1 Heat the oil and butter in a large flameproof casserole and fry the shallots, carrots, parsnips and turnips gently for 4–5 minutes.

2 Add the potatoes, pearl barley, stock, white wine and chopped mixed herbs. Bring to the boil, then cover the casserole and place it in a pre-heated oven at 190°C, 375°F, Gas Mark 5. Cook for about 1 hour, adding the sugar snap peas or mangetout (snow peas) 20 minutes before the end of the cooking time. Season to taste just before serving.

Serve in large warmed soup bowls with some crusty bread, or as a side dish to a main meal of roast or braised meat.

CORNED BEEF HASH
WITH EGGS

A quick and simple corned beef hash makes a tasty light lunch. This version uses eggs to make it more filling and nutritious.

SERVES ❹

3 tbsp vegetable oil

2 onions, chopped

1 kg/2 lb potatoes, cut into small chunks

350 g/12 oz/1½ cups corned beef (canned), cut into small cubes

few drops of Worcestershire sauce

4 eggs

salt and pepper

chopped fresh parsley to garnish

1 Heat the vegetable oil in a large frying pan (skillet) and add the onions and potatoes. Fry briskly for 2–3 minutes, then reduce the heat to low and cook gently, stirring occasionally, until the potatoes are tender – about 15–20 minutes.

2 Add the corned beef to the pan. Stir to combine and cook gently for 5 minutes, stirring occasionally. Add Worcestershire sauce and season to taste.

3 Make 4 hollows in the potato mixture and crack an egg into each one, being careful not to break the yolks. Continue to cook gently over a low heat for 4–5 minutes, until the egg whites are cooked but the yolks are still soft.

4 Divide the hash into 4, 1 egg per portion, and use a fish slice to lift each portion out on to a warmed serving plate. Garnish with a little chopped parsley.

BEEF AND ALE STEW WITH PARSLEY DUMPLINGS

The parsley dumplings taste just right in this delicious beef stew, but you must use fresh parsley, as dried doesn't have enough flavour.

SERVES ❹

1 tbsp vegetable oil

750 g/1½ lb lean stewing steak, cut into large chunks

2 celery sticks, chopped

1 large carrot, sliced

2 leeks, trimmed and sliced

450 ml/¾ pint/scant 2 cups beef stock

300 ml/½ pint/1¼ cups light ale (beer)

salt and pepper

DUMPLINGS

125 g/4 oz/1 cup self-raising flour

60 g/2 oz/¼ cup margarine

1 tbsp chopped fresh parsley

1 Heat the oil in a large saucepan. Add the chunks of meat, a handful at a time, and cook over a high heat until they are sealed and browned. Add the celery, carrot and leeks and cook for about 5 minutes, stirring frequently.

2 Pour in the beef stock and ale (beer). Season to taste. Bring to the boil, then reduce the heat. Cover and cook for about 1½–2 hours until the meat is tender.

3 To make the dumplings, sift the flour and a pinch of salt into a mixing bowl. Stir in the chopped parsley and rub in the margarine with your fingertips until the mixture resembles fine breadcrumbs. Add sufficient chilled water to make a soft, but not sticky, dough. Form into 8 dumplings and add them to the beef mixture.

18

4 Cover the saucepan and simmer for about 20 minutes until the dumplings are cooked – they should be light and fluffy.

Serve at once, accompanied by fresh vegetables and mashed potatoes.

STEAK AND KIDNEY PUDDING

SERVES ❹

350 g/12 oz/3 cups self-raising flour

175 g/6 oz/1¼ cups shredded beef suet

30 g/1 oz/¼ cup plain (all-purpose) flour

500 g/1 lb braising steak, trimmed and cut into 2.5 cm/ 1 inch chunks

125 g/4 oz/½ cup ox kidney, trimmed and chopped

1 small onion, chopped

125 g/4 oz/1 cup open-cup mushrooms, wiped and sliced

few drops of mushroom ketchup (catsup) or Worcestershire sauce

salt and pepper

Allow plenty of time when you begin to make this traditional savoury pudding, as it needs several hours to steam to perfection.

1 Grease a 1.25 litre/ 2¼ pint/5 cup pudding basin with margarine.

2 Sift the self-raising flour and a pinch of salt into a large mixing bowl. Stir in the shredded beef suet and add sufficient chilled water to make a soft, but not sticky, dough.

3 On a lightly floured work surface (counter) roll out about three quarters of the dough and use it to line the greased pudding basin.

4 Sprinkle the plain (all-purpose) flour on to a large plate and season. Roll the steak and kidney pieces, onion and mushrooms in the flour, then put into the dough-lined basin. Sprinkle with a few drops of mushroom ketchup (catsup) or Worcestershire sauce, then add just enough cold water to reach the top of the meat.

5 Roll out the remaining dough to form a lid for the pudding basin. Moisten the edges and position over the meat

mixture, pressing the edges of the dough together well to seal them. Cover with a large piece of greaseproof (waxed) paper or foil and secure with string.

6 Put the pudding basin in a steamer over a pan of gently boiling water and steam for about 4¹/2 hours, adding more boiling water when necessary to prevent the steamer from boiling dry. Serve with carrots, cabbage or Brussels sprouts and boiled or mashed potatoes.

BRAISED BRISKET OF BEEF

SERVES 6

2 tbsp vegetable oil

1.25 kg/2½ lb piece of brisket of beef, rolled and tied

250 g/8 oz small onions, halved

300 ml/½ pint/1¼ cups beef stock

300 ml/½ pint/1¼ cups red wine

2 bay leaves

6 juniper berries

1 tbsp chopped fresh parsley

15 g/½ oz/2 tbsp cornflour (cornstarch), blended with a little cold water

salt and pepper

Brisket of beef is a delicious cut of meat, especially when slow-cooked in the oven. The red wine and juniper berries add a distinctive but subtle flavour.

1 Heat the vegetable oil in a large flameproof casserole. Add the piece of brisket and cook over a high heat, turning it to seal and brown on all sides.

2 Add the onions, beef stock, red wine, bay leaves, juniper berries and parsley. Season to taste. Bring to the boil, then cover the casserole.

3 Place the casserole in a preheated oven at 160°C, 325°F, Gas Mark 3, and cook for about 2 hours until the meat is tender, basting it occasionally. Remove the brisket from the casserole and leave to rest for about 5 minutes.

4 Add the blended cornflour (cornstarch) to the gravy in the casserole and stir well. Bring to the boil over a low heat, stirring constantly until it is thickened and blended. Cook gently for 2 minutes. Carve the meat and serve with a jugful of the gravy, accompanied by potatoes and fresh vegetables.

22

ROAST LAMB WITH ONION SAUCE

Garlic and rosemary give a subtle flavour to roast lamb, which in this recipe is served with an onion sauce as a pleasant change to mint sauce or gravy.

SERVES 6

1.5–1.75 kg/3–3½ lb leg of lamb (fillet end)

2 large garlic cloves, cut into slivers

sprigs of fresh rosemary

30 g/1 oz/2 tbsp butter

sprigs of fresh rosemary to garnish

SAUCE

30 g/1 oz/2 tbsp butter

1 large onion, chopped finely

30 g/1 oz/¼ cup plain (all-purpose) flour

200 ml/7 fl oz/generous ¾ cup milk

150 ml/¼ pint/⅔ cup lamb or vegetable stock

pinch of ground allspice

salt and pepper

1 Using a sharp knife, make small incisions over the surface of the lamb. Insert the slivers of garlic and some tiny sprigs of rosemary. Spread the butter over the lamb.

2 Transfer to a roasting tin (pan) and place in a preheated oven at 220°C, 425°F, Gas Mark 7. Roast for 30 minutes, then reduce the temperature to 180°C, 350°F, Gas Mark 4 and cook for a further 1½–1¾ hours.

3 About 20 minutes before the end of the cooking time, make the onion sauce. Melt the butter in a saucepan and add the onion. Cook very gently over a low heat for about 10 minutes, until softened but not brown, stirring occasionally. Stir in the flour and cook gently for 1 minute, then add the milk and stock gradually, stirring well

24

between each addition. Bring to the boil, stirring constantly until smooth and thickened. Add a pinch of allspice, and season.

Carve the lamb and serve with potatoes, vegetables and the onion sauce. Garnish with sprigs of fresh rosemary.

RABBIT CASSEROLE WITH MUSTARD AND BACON

SERVES 6

1 kg/2 lb rabbit pieces

30 g/1 oz/¼ cup plain (all-purpose) flour

30 g/1 oz/2 tbsp butter

1 tbsp vegetable oil

125 g/4 oz/½ cup thick-cut streaky (fatty) bacon, chopped

175 g/6 oz shallots

2 celery sticks, sliced

300 ml/½ pint/1¼ cups dry white wine

150 ml/¼ pint/⅔ cup chicken or vegetable stock

1 tbsp wholegrain mustard

1 bay leaf

salt and pepper

Rabbit makes a welcome change from other meats or poultry and tastes particularly good with this combination of white wine and bacon.

1 Rinse the rabbit pieces and pat dry with paper towels. Dust with the flour.

2 Heat the butter and oil in a large frying pan (skillet) and add the rabbit. Cook over a fairly high heat to brown and seal them, then transfer to a large casserole.

3 Add the bacon to the frying pan (skillet) and cook until the fat begins to run, then transfer to the casserole. Fry the shallots gently in the bacon fat, then add to the casserole with the celery.

4 Pour the white wine into the frying pan (skillet) and bring to the boil, stirring well to combine with the pan juices. Pour into the casserole with the stock. Stir in the wholegrain mustard and season to taste. Add the bay leaf.

5 Cover the casserole and cook in a preheated oven at 190°C, 375°F, Gas Mark 5, for 1½–2 hours until very tender.

26

POT-ROASTED CHICKEN

SERVES 4

30 g/1 oz/2 tbsp butter

1 tbsp vegetable oil

125 g/4 oz/½ cup smoked streaky (fatty) bacon, de-rinded and chopped

1.5–1.75 kg/3–3½ lb chicken

1 large onion, sliced

1 large carrot, sliced

1 small lemon, halved

300 ml/½ pint/1¼ cups dry white wine

300 ml/½ pint/1¼ cups chicken stock

small bunch of fresh herbs, tied in a bundle

15 g/½ oz/2 tbsp cornflour (cornstarch), blended with a little cold water

Pot-roasted chicken is exceptionally succulent, and a lemon placed in the cavity of the bird gives it a lovely flavour. For a slightly different flavour, use red wine instead of white and add 125g/4 oz/1 cup button mushrooms to the casserole.

1 Heat the butter and oil in a large flameproof casserole and fry the bacon until the fat runs. Remove the bacon and set it aside.

2 Put the chicken in the casserole and fry it over a fairly high heat, turning it over to brown on all sides. Remove the chicken and set it aside.

3 Fry the sliced onion and carrot in the casserole for 3–4 minutes, until lightly browned.

4 Push the lemon halves into the cavity of the chicken and return to the casserole with the bacon. Pour in the wine and stock and bring to the boil. Then turn off the heat, add the bundle of herbs and cover the casserole with a piece of foil.

5 Place the casserole in a preheated oven at 190°C, 375°F, Gas Mark 5, and cook for 1½–2 hours, basting occasionally with the stock.

28

6 When the chicken is cooked, remove it from the casserole, draining it well. Discard the herbs and lemon halves.

7 Add the blended cornflour (cornstarch) to the cooking liquid, stirring to mix. Cook over a gentle heat, stirring constantly until thickened and blended. Cook for 1 minute, then serve with the chicken.

TOAD-IN-THE-HOLE

Serve this straight from the oven, all puffed up and golden brown. The mushroom and onion gravy complements it perfectly.

SERVES ❹

125 g/4 oz/1 cup plain (all-purpose) flour

½ tsp dried thyme

1 large egg (size 1)

300 ml/½ pint/1¼ cups milk

2 tbsp vegetable oil

500 g/1 lb pork sausages

GRAVY

15 g/½ oz/1 tbsp butter or margarine

1 small onion, chopped finely

60 g/2 oz/½ cup button mushrooms, sliced thinly

450 ml/¾ pint/scant 2 cups vegetable or chicken stock

15g/½ oz/2 tbsp cornflour (cornstarch) blended with a little cold water

salt and pepper

1 Sift the flour and a pinch of salt into a large mixing bowl. Add the herbs, egg and milk and, using a balloon whisk or electric hand mixer, beat together to make a smooth batter. Set aside for 10–15 minutes before using.

2 Meanwhile, pour the oil into a roasting tin (pan) and arrange the sausages in the base. Place in a preheated oven at 220°C, 425°F, Gas Mark 7, for 10 minutes so that the oil gets very hot.

3 Remove from the oven, pour in the batter quickly and return to the oven. (It is important to pour the batter into very hot oil and return it to the oven immediately.) Cook for 25–30 minutes until the batter is well risen and golden brown.

4 While this is cooking, make the gravy. Melt the margarine or butter in a saucepan and fry the onion gently for about 8–10 minutes until well

30

browned. Add the mushrooms and cook for a further 2 minutes. Pour in the stock and bring to the boil, then reduce the heat and simmer gently for 10 minutes. Add the blended cornflour (cornstarch) and cook, stirring, for about 2 minutes, until thickened and smooth. Season to taste. Divide the cooked toad-in-the-hole into 4 portions and serve with the gravy and some fresh vegetables.

PORK, SAUSAGES AND BEANS

SERVES ❹

90 g/3 oz haricot (navy) beans, soaked overnight

90 g/3 oz black-eye beans (peas), soaked overnight

350 g/12 oz belly pork, de-rinded

350 g/12 oz pork sausages

1 tbsp vegetable oil

1 large onion, chopped

1 large carrot, chopped

450 ml/³⁄₄ pint/scant 2 cups ham, chicken or vegetable stock

30 g/1 oz/2 tbsp dark muscovado or molasses sugar

2 tbsp tomato purée (paste)

1 tbsp chopped fresh herbs

2 tsp chopped fresh root ginger

400 g/14 oz can tomatoes

2 tbsp cornflour (cornstarch) mixed with a little cold water

This warming casserole of belly pork, pork sausages and beans is farmhouse cookery at its best – a simple and inexpensive dish full of flavour and goodness.

1 Drain the beans and rinse well with fresh water. Place the beans in a large saucepan of water, bring to the boil and boil rapidly for 10 minutes. Drain.

2 Cut the meat into 2.5 cm/ 1 inch cubes. Twist the sausages in the middle and snip them in half.

3 Heat the oil in a large flameproof casserole and add the belly pork, cooking over a high heat until beginning to brown on all sides. Add the sausages and fry gently for a few more minutes until browned. Add the onion and carrot and cook for 2–3 minutes to soften. Add the stock, sugar, tomato purée (paste), herbs and ginger, and chop up and stir in the tomatoes. Season to taste.

4 Cover the casserole, place in a preheated

oven at 160°C, 325°F, Gas Mark 3, and cook for 2–2¹/₂ hours until the pork is tender and the beans are soft. Stir in the blended cornflour (cornstarch). Return to the oven for a further 5 minutes to cook and thicken before serving.

CRISPY-TOPPED FISH PIE

A crisp and golden topping of cheesy potatoes conceals a layer of cod in a creamy parsley sauce in this easy and tasty fish recipe.

SERVES ❹

45 g/1½ oz/3 tbsp butter or margarine
....
750 g/1½ lb potatoes
....
1 bunch spring onions (scallions), trimmed and chopped finely
....
45 g/1½ oz/⅓ cup plain (all-purpose) flour
....
300 ml/½ pint/1¼ cups milk
....
1 tbsp chopped fresh parsley
....
750 g/1½ lb cod or haddock, skinned, boned and cut into chunks
....
1 egg
....
150 ml/¼ pint/⅔ cup natural yogurt
....
125 g/4 oz/1 cup mature (sharp) Cheddar cheese, grated
....
salt and black pepper
....

1 Grease a 1.5 litre/2½ pint/1½ quart ovenproof dish with a little of the butter or margarine.

2 Cook the potatoes in plenty of boiling, lightly salted water until just tender. Drain and slice.

3 Melt the remaining butter or margarine in a saucepan and fry the spring onions (scallions) gently until softened. Remove the saucepan from the heat and stir in the flour. Then cook over a low heat for 1 minute and add the milk gradually. Bring to the boil, stirring constantly. Cook until smooth and thick. Add the parsley and season to taste. Stir in the fish.

4 Transfer the mixture to the greased baking dish and arrange the sliced potatoes over the top in an overlapping layer.

5 Beat together the egg and yogurt. Add half the cheese and season to taste. Pour over the potatoes and sprinkle with

the remaining cheese. Bake in a preheated oven at 190°C, 375°F, Gas Mark 5 for 25–30 minutes until set and golden brown.

Serve at once, with lightly cooked fresh vegetables or a salad.

TROUT WITH LEMON AND HERB MARINADE

Fish lends itself well to simple methods of cooking, as this recipe for trout marinated in a lemon, garlic and herb mixture proves.

SERVES ❹

4 trout, cleaned and gutted

finely grated rind of 1 large lemon

4 tbsp lemon juice

4 tbsp olive oil

1 large garlic clove, crushed

1 tbsp chopped fresh marjoram

1 tbsp chopped fresh parsley (flat leaf or curly)

salt and pepper

1 Rinse the trout well, then use a sharp knife to make 2 or 3 slashes on each side of the fish, in the thickest part of the flesh. Place in a shallow, non-metallic container.

2 Mix together the lemon rind and juice, olive oil, garlic, marjoram and parsley. Season to taste, then pour the mixture over the fish. Cover and leave to marinate for 2–3 hours.

3 Place the fish on a pre-heated hot grill (broiler) rack and cook for about 5 minutes each side, basting frequently with the lemon and herb mixture. The fish is cooked when the flesh is opaque and flakes easily.

Serve at once, accompanied by new (baby) potatoes and a selection of fresh vegetables, or a green salad.

SALMON FISH CAKES WITH DILL SAUCE

Fish cakes take on a new meaning with this special recipe, which uses fresh salmon and dill. Smoked haddock or cod can be used for a more economical version.

SERVES ❹

500 g/1 lb potatoes, cut into large chunks

350 g/12 oz salmon fillets or steaks

sprigs of fresh dill or parsley

2 tsp white wine vinegar

60 g/2 oz/¼ cup butter

150 ml/¼ pint/⅔ cup single (light) cream

2 tsp lemon juice

2 tsp chopped fresh dill or parsley

45 g/1½ oz/¼ cup plus 2 tbsp plain (all-purpose) flour

1 egg, separated

90 g/3 oz/1½ cups fresh white breadcrumbs

butter and vegetable oil

salt and pepper

1 Cook the potatoes in plenty of boiling, lightly salted water until tender. Drain well and mash them.

2 While the potatoes are cooking, place the salmon in a shallow pan with the sprigs of dill or parsley and the vinegar. Pour in just enough water to cover. Place the pan over a low heat and simmer gently to poach the fish. When cooked, the fish should be opaque and will flake easily. Drain well, reserving the poaching liquid. Flake the fish with a fork, removing any skin and bones.

3 Mix together the potatoes and fish with 30 g/1 oz/ 2 tbsp of the butter, 3 tbsp of the single (light) cream, the lemon juice and 1 tsp of the chopped dill or parsley. Season to taste.

4 Form the mixture into 8 cakes and dust with 30 g/1 oz/¼ cup of the flour. Beat the egg white in a shallow bowl with 1 tbsp cold water. Put the breadcrumbs on to a separate plate. Dip the fish cakes in the egg white, then coat with the

breadcrumbs. Fry in butter and vegetable oil until cooked and golden brown, about 4–5 minutes on each side.

5 To make the sauce, put the remaining butter, cream, dill or parsley, egg yolk, flour and 4 tbsp of the poaching liquid into a small saucepan. Heat, stirring constantly with a balloon whisk, until thickened and smooth.

Serve with the fish cakes.

GOLDEN POTATO CAKES

Served with sizzling bacon and fresh eggs for breakfast, these potato cakes are delicious.

SERVES ❹

1 kg/2 lb cooked potatoes

60 g/2 oz/¼ cup butter

1 egg, beaten

90 g/3 oz/¾ cup plain (all-purpose) flour

1 tbsp vegetable oil

salt and pepper

1 Mash the potatoes with 45 g/1½ oz/ 3 tbsp of the butter, then beat well until smooth, using an electric hand mixer for the best results. Add the egg and 60 g/2 oz/½ cup of the flour, beating well until thoroughly blended. Season well to taste.

2 On a lightly floured work surface (counter), use a rolling pin to press and roll the mixture out gently until it forms a circle about 25 cm/10 inches in diameter. Cut into large wedges and dust with the remaining flour.

3 Heat the oil with the remaining butter in a large heavy-based frying pan (skillet). Add the potato cakes and cook over a gentle heat for about 4–5 minutes. Turn over carefully and cook the other side until golden brown. Drain on paper towels before serving.

BAKED STUFFED ONIONS

Use mildly flavoured onions to make this economical recipe. Be sure to make full use of the oven by cooking another dish at the same time – why not bake some potatoes to serve with the onions?

1 Grease an ovenproof dish with butter.

2 Put the onions into a large saucepan of lightly salted water. Bring to the boil, reduce the heat and cook for 15 minutes. Drain and cool slightly, then hollow out the centres and chop them finely.

3 Fry the bacon in a medium frying pan (skillet) until the fat runs. Add the minced (ground) beef, chopped onion and mushrooms and cook for 8–10 minutes over a medium heat, stirring frequently. Remove from the heat and stir in the breadcrumbs and herbs. Season to taste.

4 Stand the whole onions in the greased ovenproof dish. Pack the minced (ground) beef mixture into the centres and pour the stock around them. Place in a preheated oven at 180°C, 350°F, Gas Mark 4, and bake for 1½–2 hours until tender.

BUBBLE AND SQUEAK

Excellent served with chops, bacon, ham or sausages, Bubble and Squeak is a traditional way of using up leftover potatoes. A couple of teaspoons of wholegrain mustard can be added to the mixture.

SERVES 4

1 small onion, chopped

1 small cabbage, shredded

500 g/1 lb cooked potatoes

30 g/1 oz/2 tbsp butter

1 tbsp chopped fresh chives or parsley

60 g/2 oz/½ cup plain (all-purpose) flour

3 tbsp vegetable oil

salt and pepper

1 Put the onion and cabbage into a large saucepan with a little boiling, lightly salted water. Cover and cook for about 5–6 minutes, until tender. Drain the vegetables well.

2 While the vegetables are cooking, beat the cooked potatoes and butter together until smooth, using either a wooden spoon or, preferably, an electric hand mixer for best results. Add the chives or parsley, then mix in the cooked onion and cabbage.

3 Season well, then form the mixture into 8 rectangular cakes. Sift the flour on to a plate and use to coat the cakes lightly.

4 Heat the vegetable oil in a large frying pan (skillet) and fry the cakes gently for about 4 minutes on each side, until cooked and golden brown. Drain on paper towels and serve at once.

GREEN TOMATO CHUTNEY

Make the most of the last of the summer tomatoes in this robust chutney. It's the ideal accompaniment to fine Cheddar cheese or home-cooked ham.

MAKES 1.5kg/3lb

1 kg/2 lb green tomatoes, chopped

250 g/8 oz/2 cups onions, chopped

250 g/8 oz cooking apples, peeled, cored and chopped

125 g/4 oz/⅔ cup sultanas (golden raisins)

300 ml/½ pint/1¼ cups light malt vinegar

175 g/6 oz/1 cup light muscovado sugar

2 tsp grated fresh root ginger

1 tsp mustard seeds

2 tsp salt

½ tsp pepper

1 Sterilize 3 x 500 g/1 lb glass jars by one of the following methods: wash jars in hot soapy water and rinse in boiling water, turn upside down on a clean tea towel (dish cloth) to dry and then place in a cool oven for about 15 minutes; or wash in the dishwasher and remove just before filling; or quarter fill jars with water, microwave on full power, then pour out the water and leave jars to dry upside down on a tea towel (dish cloth).

2 Put the tomatoes, onions, apples, sultanas (golden raisins) and vinegar into a saucepan. Bring to the boil, reduce the heat and simmer for about 5 minutes. Stir in the sugar and allow to dissolve. Add the ginger, mustard seeds, salt and pepper.

3 Simmer, uncovered, stirring occasionally until the mixture becomes thick and

46

pulpy. The chutney must have quite a thick consistency, as it thickens only slightly as it cools.

4 Pot the chutney in warmed, sterilized jars. Seal and label.

SUMMER PUDDING

This beautiful dessert is a treat served in the summer months when the soft fruit you need is available. Serve it with a dollop of fresh whipped cream or natural fromage frais.

SERVES 6

250 g/8 oz/1⅓ cups strawberries, hulled

250 g/8 oz/1⅓ cups raspberries

125 g/4 oz/1 cup redcurrants

125 g/4 oz/1 cup blackcurrants

125 g/4 oz/½ cup caster (superfine) sugar

6–7 medium-thick slices white bread, crusts removed

whipped cream or fromage frais to serve

1 Grease a 900 ml/1½ pint/3½ cup pudding basin with a little butter.

2 Rinse the fruit, then slice the strawberries and put them into a saucepan with the raspberries. Use a fork to carefully strip the redcurrants and blackcurrants from their stalks, then add the fruit to the saucepan with the sugar.

3 Heat gently so that the sugar dissolves and the juice begins to run from the fruit, about 3–4 minutes. Remove the saucepan from the heat.

4 Line the basin with the bread, reserving some for the top. Press the edges together and use small pieces of bread to fill up any gaps.

5 Reserve 4 tbsp of the juice from the fruit. Pour the fruit and remaining juice into the prepared basin, and cover with the reserved bread. Place a saucer or small plate on top of the basin to fit as closely as possible, then place a heavy weight on top. Refrigerate for 6–8 hours, or overnight.

6 When ready to serve, turn the pudding out on to a large plate. Use the reserved fruit juice to spoon over any patches of bread that remain white.

Cut into wedges and serve with whipped cream or natural fromage frais.

APPLE AND BLACKBERRY PIE

SERVES 6

500 g/1 lb baking apples, peeled, cored and chopped

2 tsp lemon juice

250 g/8 oz/2 cups blackberries

90 g/3 oz/½ cup soft brown sugar

175 g/6 oz/1½ cups self-raising flour

pinch of salt

½ tsp ground cinnamon

50 g/2 oz/¼ cup butter or margarine

1 egg, beaten

3 tbsp milk

demerara sugar (sugar crystals), for sprinkling

Apples and blackberries are a winning combination. Try them in this single-crust pie, excellent served with cream, custard, ice cream or natural yogurt.

1 Grease a 1.25 litre/ 2¼ pint/1½ quart deep ovenproof dish with a little butter.

2 Put the apples into a saucepan with a little water and the lemon juice. Remove any stalks or leaves from the blackberries and add to the pan with 50 g/2 oz/⅓ cup of the soft brown sugar. Simmer gently over a low heat for 10 minutes. Allow the mixture to cool slightly before spooning it into the greased ovenproof dish.

3 Sift the flour, salt and cinnamon into a mixing bowl and stir in the remaining soft brown sugar. Rub in the butter or margarine with your fingertips until the mixture resembles fine breadcrumbs. Beat the egg and milk together, then add enough to the flour mixture to make a soft, but not sticky, dough. Knead lightly for a few moments, then chill for 5–10 minutes.

4 Roll out the dough to fit the top of the dish. Lift on to the dish, trim the edges and use any

trimmings to make leaves for decorating the top. Brush the dough with any remaining egg and milk mixture to glaze. Sprinkle with demerara sugar (sugar crystals).

5 Place in a preheated oven at 200°C, 400°F, Gas Mark 6 and bake for 20–25 minutes until cooked and golden brown.

FARMHOUSE CURD TART

Fresh dairy ingredients are the making of this lovely lemon-flavoured cheesecake tart – a favourite dessert for those who prefer their puddings not too sweet.

SERVES 6

250 g/8 oz/2 cups plain (all-purpose) flour

pinch of salt

125 g/4 oz/½ cup butter or hard margarine, chilled

single (light) cream, to serve

FILLING

3 eggs, beaten

50 ml/2 fl oz/¼ cup single (light) cream

250 g/8 oz/1 cup cottage cheese

30 g/1 oz/2 tbsp caster (superfine) sugar

few drops of vanilla flavouring (extract)

60 g/2 oz/⅓ cup currants

finely grated rind of 1 large lemon

pinch of ground nutmeg

1 Sift the flour and salt into a large mixing bowl. Cut the butter or margarine into pieces, add to the flour and rub in with your fingertips until the mixture resembles fine breadcrumbs. Stir in enough chilled water to make a firm dough. Knead lightly for a few moments, then cover in clingfilm (plastic wrap) and refrigerate for about 10 minutes.

2 Roll out the chilled dough on a lightly floured work surface (counter), and use to line a 23 cm/9 inch pie plate or flan dish. Prick the base with a fork and line with foil. Place in a preheated oven at 220°C, 425°F, Gas Mark 7, and bake for 10 minutes. Remove from the oven, take off the foil and allow the pastry to cool a little. Reduce the heat to 180°C, 350°F, Gas Mark 4.

3 To make the filling, beat together the eggs and cream. Add the cottage cheese,

caster sugar, vanilla flavouring (extract), currants and lemon rind. Pour into the pastry case and sprinkle with nutmeg.

4 Bake the tart for about 35 minutes, until the filling sets

and turns a light golden brown. Allow to cool slightly before serving with a jug of single (light) cream.

CHEESE AND FRESH HERB SCONES

MAKES 16

500 g/1 lb/4 cups self-raising flour

pinch of salt

125 g/4 oz/½ cup butter or margarine

175 g/6 oz/1½ cups mature (sharp) Cheddar cheese, grated

2 tbsp chopped fresh mixed herbs, such as chervil, chives, marjoram, mint, parsley, sage and thyme.

2 eggs

300 ml/½ pint/1¼ cups milk

Hot from the oven, these delicious scones are fragrant with the aroma of fresh herbs and cheese. Serve them while still warm, split and spread with butter.

1 Brush 2 baking sheets with a little oil.

2 Sift the flour and salt together into a large mixing bowl, then rub in the butter or margarine with your fingertips until the mixture resembles fine breadcrumbs. Stir in 125 g/4 oz/1 cup of the grated cheese and the herbs.

3 Beat together the eggs and milk, then add most of the liquid to the cheese mixture. Draw together to make a soft, but not sticky, dough and knead lightly for a few moments until smooth.

4 Roll the dough out on a lightly floured work surface (counter) to a thickness of 2.5cm/1 inch. Use a 5 cm/2 inch pastry cutter to stamp out rounds. Place on the baking sheets, brush with the remaining egg and milk mixture, and sprinkle the remaining cheese on top.

5 Place in a preheated oven at 220°C, 425°F, Gas Mark 7, and bake until risen and golden brown, about 10–12 minutes.

Transfer to a wire rack to cool slightly. Serve warm, spread with butter.

SULTANA DROP SCONES

Drop scones, or Scotch pancakes as they are sometimes known, get their name from the way that the batter is dropped on to a hot griddle – although a heavy-based frying pan (skillet) can easily be used instead.

MAKES 18

125 g/4 oz/1 cup self-raising flour

pinch of salt

15 g/½ oz/1 heaped tbsp soft brown sugar

1 egg

1 tsp vanilla flavouring (extract)

½ tsp finely grated orange rind

150 ml/¼ pint/⅔ cup natural yogurt

2 tbsp milk

30 g/1 oz/3 tbsp sultanas (golden raisins) or raisins

few drops of vegetable oil

1 Sift the flour and salt into a mixing bowl. Stir in the sugar. Add the egg, vanilla flavouring (extract), orange rind, yogurt and milk and beat together using a wire whisk until the batter is smooth. Stir in the sultanas (golden raisins) or raisins.

2 Heat a griddle or heavy-based frying pan (skillet), adding just a few drops of oil to grease the surface. Turn the heat to low. Drop tablespoonfuls of the batter on to the hot surface, allowing space for each spoonful to spread out a little. When air-bubbles appear on the surface of the scones after about 2 minutes, flip each scone over and cook for a further 2 minutes. Using a fish slice, lift them out on to paper towels or a clean tea towel (dish cloth), then cook the remaining batter, adding a few more drops of oil to the pan if necessary.

These are best served warm, spread with butter.

WHOLEWHEAT FRUIT TEABREAD

This easy-to-make fruit teabread is best served in slices spread with butter, and is ideal for taking on picnics.

1 Grease a 1 kg/2 lb loaf tin (pan) with a little vegetable oil. Line with greaseproof paper (baking parchment).

2 Sift the flour, salt and mixed spice into a mixing bowl, adding any bits of bran that remain in the sieve. Stir in the sugar, then rub in the butter or margarine with your fingertips until the mixture resembles fine breadcrumbs.

3 Beat together the eggs and milk and add to the mixture with the dates, apricots and sultanas (golden raisins), stirring well to mix thoroughly.

4 Turn the mixture into the prepared tin (pan) and level the surface. Place in a preheated oven at 160°C, 325°F, Gas Mark 3, and bake for about 1 hour 10 minutes until risen and

golden brown. To test if the teabread is cooked, insert a skewer into the centre – it should come out clean.

5 Cool the teabread in the tin (pan) for 10 minutes, then transfer to a wire rack to cool completely before slicing.

BLACKCURRANT PRESERVE

Make the most of soft summer fruit with this wonderful preserve. Blackcurrants are ideal because they have a high pectin content, which helps the preserve to set.

1 Sterilize 6 x 500 g/1 lb glass jars (see page 46).

2 Check over the fruit to remove any stalks and leaves, but avoid washing the fruit unless really necessary.

3 Put the fruit into a preserving pan or very large saucepan with the water. Simmer gently over a low heat for 30–40 minutes to soften the fruit and release the pectin.

4 Add the sugar to the blackcurrants and allow it to dissolve, stirring occasionally. Bring to the boil and boil rapidly until setting point is reached (see below) – about 15–20 minutes. Skim off any scum, but not foam, near the end of the cooking time.

5 To test for setting-point, spoon a little of the mixture on to a cold saucer and cool it quickly. Push it with your finger – it should crinkle on the surface, but should not be stiff. Double-check by putting a drop of the

cooled preserve on the end of your finger. If it does not fall off, it is ready.

6 Pot the preserve in the warmed, sterilized jars, seal and label. It will set as it cools.

LEMON CURD

MAKES 750g / 1 ½ lb
4 eggs
250 g/8 oz/1 firmly packed cup caster (superfine) sugar
finely grated rind of 2 large lemons
120 ml/4 fl oz/½ cup lemon juice
250 g/8 oz/1 cup unsalted butter, melted

Fresh homemade lemon curd is a real treat, especially when spread generously on to crusty new bread. Remember to refrigerate and eat within 3 weeks – although there should be no problem in doing that!

1 Sterilize 2 x 350 g/ 12 oz glass jars (see page 46).

2 Whisk together the eggs, sugar, lemon rind and juice in a heatproof mixing bowl. Add the warm melted butter and stir together.

3 Set the bowl over a pan of gently simmering water and stir with a wooden spoon until the mixture thickens, about 10–15 minutes. Check that it is thick enough by lifting the wooden spoon a little and drizzling the lemon curd over the surface of the mixture – it should be thick enough to leave a trail. The lemon curd will thicken more as it cools.

4 Pot the lemon curd in warmed sterilized jars. Seal and label. When completely cool, store in the refrigerator.

INDEX